It's fun to draw

All Things

Big and Small

It's fun to draw

All Things
Big and Small

Mark Bergin

Sky Pony Press
New York

Author:
Mark Bergin was born in Hastings, England.
He has illustrated an award-winning series and
written over twenty books. He has done many book
designs, layouts, and storyboards in many styles
including cartoon for numerous books, posters, and
adverts. He lives in Bexhill-on-Sea with his wife
and three children.

HOW TO USE THIS BOOK:
Start by following the numbered splats on the left-
hand page. These steps will ask you to add some
lines to your drawing. The new lines are always
drawn in red so you can see how the drawing builds
from step to step. Read the "You can do it!" splats
to learn about drawing and shading techniques you
can use.

Previously published separately as *It's Fun to Draw Creepy-
Crawlies* 978-1-63220-406-6 and *It's Fun to Draw Dinosaurs and
Other Prehistoric Creatures* 978-1-61608-478-3

Sky Pony Press books may be purchased in bulk at special discounts
for sales promotion, corporate gifts, fund-raising, or educational
purposes. Special editions can also be created to specifications.
For details, contact the Special Sales Department, Sky Pony Press,
307 West 36th Street, 11th Floor, New York, NY 10018 or info@
skyhorsepublishing.com.

Sky Pony® is a registered trademark of Skyhorse Publishing, Inc.®,
a Delaware corporation.

Visit our website at www.skyponypress.com.

10 9 8 7 6 5 4 3 2 1

This product conforms to CPSIA 2008

Library of Congress Cataloging-in-Publication Data is available on
file

Cover design by Kai Texel
Cover illustrations by Mark Bergin
ISBN: 978-1-5107-7899-3
Printed in China

Contents

Contents

It's fun to draw

All Things

Big and Small

Ants

1 Start by drawing two circles.

2 Draw in the large abdomen.

3 Draw in the legs.

you can do it!

Paint the ants brown and use a darker tone for the lines. Add splattered ink for the texture.

splat-a-fact

There are more than 12,000 known species of ants.

4 Draw in the face and add lines for the antennae.

5 Add lines to the abdomen.

Bee

1 Start by drawing the head and body.

2 Add two antennae and zigzags to the body.

3 Add six legs.

Splat-a-fact
Bees make honey and beeswax.

you can do it!
Use felt-tip for the lines and add color using colored pencils.

4 Draw in the face.

5 Draw in four wings.

Mosquito

1 Start with the head and body.

2 Add the long abdomen.

3 Add the pointed feeding tube and the eyes.

4 Draw in six legs and add lines to the abdomen.

you can do it!
Use a felt-tip pen for the lines and add color using fine liners. Use straight lines, squiggly lines and cross-hatching to add interest.

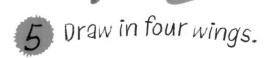

5 Draw in four wings.

Snail

1 Start with the head and long body.

splat-a-fact

Snails leave a trail of mucus as they move along.

You can do it!

Use felt-tip for the lines and then add color with watercolor paints. Dab on more color with a sponge to add texture.

2 Draw in a curly shell.

3 Draw in the face.

4 Draw in two antennae and add detail to the shell.

14

Beetle

1 Draw the body and head. The head is flat on one side.

2 Draw in six legs, each with two claws at the end.

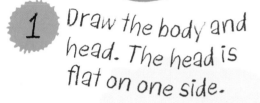

you can do it!

Draw the outlines with a black felt-tip pen. Sponge on colored inks.

splat-a-fact

Adult beetles have two sets of wings.

3 Draw in the eyes and a line down the body. Add two big mandibles (mouth parts).

16

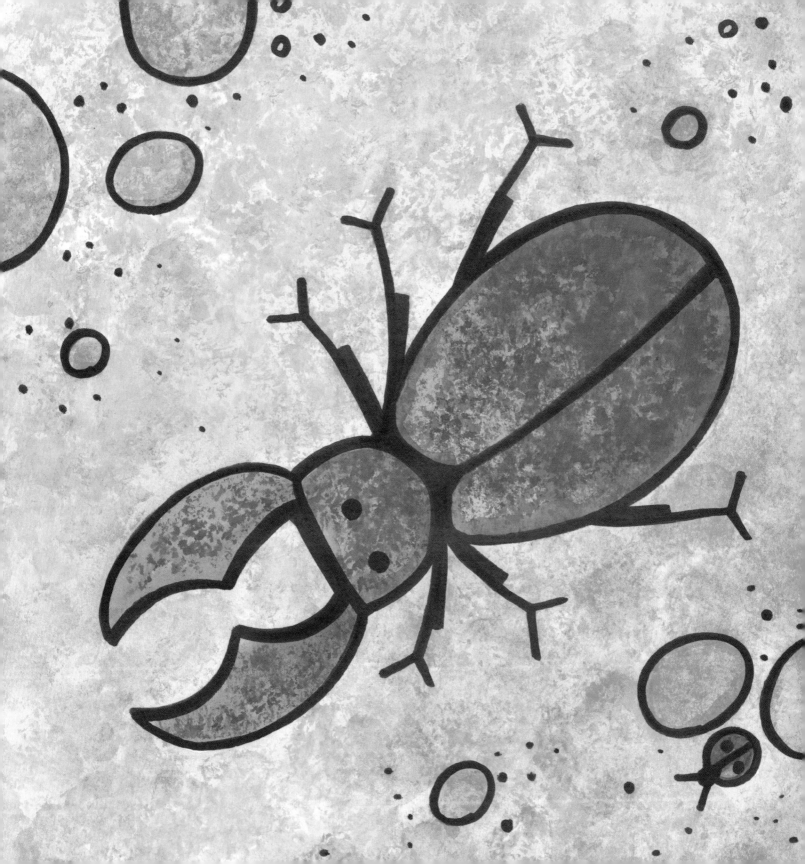

Spider

1 Start by drawing the head and body.

2 Add two large fangs and the abdomen.

you can do it!

Use a soft pencil to draw in the lines. Add color using watercolor paint.

splat-a-fact

Spiders are arachnids. They have 8 legs. Insects only have 6 legs.

3 Draw in the front four legs using curved lines.

4 Draw in the back four legs. Add dots for the eyes.

18

Dragonfly

1 Draw a body and a long abdomen.

2 Draw in the head and add six legs.

Splat- a fact
There are over 5,000 known species of dragonfly.

you can do it!
Use a felt-tip pen for the lines and a wax crayon for the detail. When you paint on top, the wax will act as a resistant.

3 Draw in two sets of wings.

4 Draw in the face. Add lines to the abdomen and wings.

Caterpillar

1 Start by drawing lots of circles for the body.

2 Add two antennae and lots of legs.

you can do it!

Use felt-tips for the lines and color in with wax crayons. Try different kinds of scribbly crayon marks to add variety. Paint over with a watercolor wash.

3 Draw in the face and add dots to the body.

Splat-a-fact

Caterpillars turn into butterflies or moths.

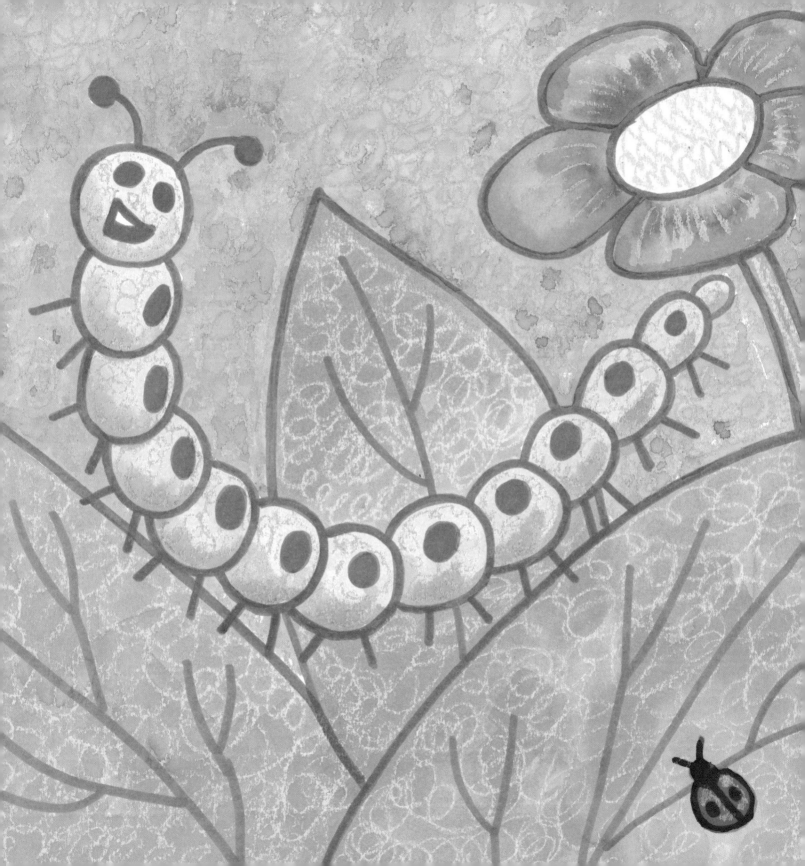

Scorpion

1 Start with the head and body.

2 Add the mouth parts and dots for the eyes.

3 Draw in the tail with a stinger at the end.

You can do it!
Use felt-tip for the lines and add color with colored oil pastels.

Splat-a-fact
Scorpions glow in ultraviolet light.

4 Draw in six legs using curved lines.

5 Draw in the front arms and claws.

Butterfly

1
Start by drawing in the body.

2 Draw in the face and and add antennae.

you can do it!

Use a blue felt-tip for the lines, then use wax crayons for coloring.

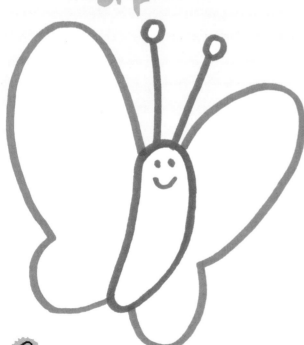

3 Draw in the wings.

4 Draw in the legs and add spots to the wings.

Moth

1 Cut out the wings and stick down.

2 Cut out six legs and stick down.

MAKE SURE AN ADULT HELPS YOU WHEN USING SCISSORS!

you can do it!
Cut out the shapes from colored paper and glue in place. Use a felt-tip for details.

Splat-a-fact
Most moths like to fly at night.

3 Cut out and stick down the abdomen, body and head.

4 Cut out and stick down the antennae and chest. Draw in head details.

Ladybird

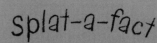

Splat-a-fact
Gardeners like ladybirds because they eat plant-eating pests.

1 Draw the head and body.

you can do it!
Draw the lines with felt-tip. Add color usng colored pencils.

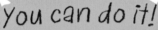

2 Add a curved line to the body and draw in six legs.

3 Draw in the face and two antennae.

4 Draw spots on the body.

30

Grasshopper

1 Start with the head and the body.

2 Add the long pointed abdomen.

you can do it!
Use a felt-tip pen for the lines. Color with pastels and blend them with your finger.

3 Draw in the face, antennae and wings.

splat-a-fact
Grasshoppers make a noise by rubbing their legs against their wings.

4 Draw in four front legs and two big back legs.

Wasp

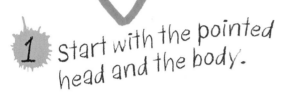

1 Start with the pointed head and the body.

2 Draw in the pointed, stripey abdomen.

splat-a-fact
Only female wasps can sting.

you can do it!
Draw the lines with a felt-tip and stick down torn tissue paper for color.

3 Add six legs and mandibles (mouth parts).

4 Draw in the face and two antennae.

5 Draw in four wings.

34

Diplodocus

Di-plod-OH-kuss

1 Start with the head.

2 Add a dot for the eye and two leaves.

3 Draw two lines for the neck.

you can do it!

Use felt-tip markers for the lines and color in with crayons, using your fingers to smudge colors together.

splat-a-fact

Diplodocus had the longest tail of any animal that has ever walked on earth.

4 Draw an oval shape for the body.

splat-a-fact

Fifteen tall men lying head to toe in a line would measure the same length as a Diplodocus.

6 Draw two long lines for a tail.

5 Draw four legs.

36

Tyrannosaurus rex

Tie-RAN-oh-sore-us

1 Draw a rectangle with a half circle.

2 Draw a smaller rectangle and another half circle.

3 Draw dots for a nose and an eye, and add zig-zag lines for teeth.

4 Add lines for the body.

5 Draw in the arms and the legs.

you can do it!

Paint the Tyrannosaurus green. Draw lines with a yellow crayon, then color in with felt-tip markers or paint. The crayon wax acts as a resistant to the paint.

Splat-a-fact

Tyrannosaurus rex means "tyrant lizard king." A large meat eater, Tyrannosaurus ate large dinosaurs like Triceratops.

Ankylosaurus

An-keel-oh-SAW-rus

1 Start with the head and eyes.

2 Add a mouth, a nostril, and three spikes.

3 Draw a big oval shape for the body.

you can do it!
Use a felt-tip marker for the lines and then add color with watercolor paints. Use a sponge to dab on more color for added texture.

4 Draw two lines for the tail, with small ovals at the end.

splat-a-fact
The Ankylosaurus could swing its big, bony tail to club its enemies.

5 Draw four legs.

6 Draw a line through the middle of the body.

7 Add spikes.

40

Pteranodon

Terr-AN-oh-don

1 Start with the head.

2 Add a tongue and a dot for the eye.

3 Draw two lines for the neck and a circle for the body.

4 Draw in the curved shape of the wings.

splat-a-fact

A Pteranodon's wings, made of leathery skin, were as large as a hang glider.

5 Add the legs and the feet.

you can do it!

Use a soft pencil for the lines and add color with watercolor paint.

42

Dimetrodon

Di-MET-ro-don

1 Start with the head.

2 Add the mouth, a nostril and a circle with a dot for the eye.

5 Draw a big curved shape with straight lines in it.

you can do it!

Use a felt-tip pen for the lines and then use colored fine-tipped markers. Use straight lines, squiggly lines, and cross-hatching to add interest.

3 Draw two lines for the neck, joined to a big oval.

4 Draw two lines to add the tail.

Splat-a-fact

A Dimetrodon's back "sail" was made of tough skin and long bones.

6 Add four legs.

44

Parasaurolophus

Para-saw-ROLL-oh-fuss

1 Start with the head with a small mouth and a dot for the eye.

2 Draw two lines for a crest and add nostrils.

3 Draw two lines for the neck, an oval shape for the body, and two curved lines for the tail.

you can do it!
Paint the Parasaurolophus yellow and pink then scribble lines with a yellow crayon. Add color with paint. The crayon wax acts as a resistant to the paint.

Splat-a-fact
Parasaurolophus had the biggest head crest of all the duck-billed dinosaurs.

4 Draw in two legs and two arms.

Pachycephalosaurus

pack-ee-seff-ah-low-saw-rus

1 Start with a head and an eye.

2 Add the mouth, a nostril, two nose spikes, and some small circles.

3 Add two lines for the neck, a big oval, two curved lines for the tail, and two arms.

Splat- a fact

A Pachycephalosaurus was the same height as a double decker bus when it stood upright to feed.

you can do it!

Use a felt-tip marker for the lines and add color with chalky pastels. Use your finger to smudge the colors.

4 Add two legs with clawed feet.

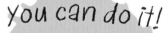

Stegosaurus

stegg-oh-SAW-rus

1 Start with the head.

2 Add the mouth and dots for the nostrils and eye.

3 Draw two lines for the neck and a circle for the body.

4 Draw two lines for the tail and add four legs.

you can do it!

Use felt-tip markers for the lines and add color with crayons. Use different kinds of scribbly crayon marks to add variety.

5 Add kite-shaped plates on its back and spikes at the end of the tail.

Splat-a-fact

Some of the Stegosaurus's back plates were about 2 feet tall and 2 feet wide.

Iguanodon

Ig-WAN-oh-don

1 Start with the head.

2 Add the mouth and dots for the eye and nostril.

3 Draw lines for the neck and an oval shape for the body.

4 Draw two lines for the tail.

5 Add two legs, two feet, and two arms.

Splat-a-fact

The Iguanadon was first found in England.

You can do it!

Use felt-tip markers for the lines and add color with watercolor paints. Make a smudged effect by adding green paint to the yellow while it is still wet.

Liopleurodon

Lee-oh-PLOOR-oh-don

1 Cut out the shape of the head.

2 Draw in the eye, nostril, and zig-zag mouth.

you can do it!

Cut out the shapes from colored paper with crayon stripes. Stick these on to a sheet of blue paper. Use felt-tip markers for the lines and white gouache for the air bubbles.

2 Cut out an oval shape for the body and a pointed tail.

3 Cut out four pointed flippers.

MAKE SURE YOU GET AN ADULT TO HELP YOU WHEN USING SCISSORS!

Splat-a-fact

Liopleurodon had strong flippers to speed through water after its prey.

4 Glue all of the body into place and add the head last to overlap.

54

styracosaurus

Sty-RACK-o-saw-rus

1 Start with the head: add spikes, a horn, an eye, and a mouth.

2 Draw a circle for the body.

Splat-a-fact
Styracosaurus means "spiked lizard."

3 Draw two curved lines for the tail.

you can do it!
Use felt-tip markers for the lines and color in with oil pastels. Smudge colors together with your finger.

4 Add four legs.

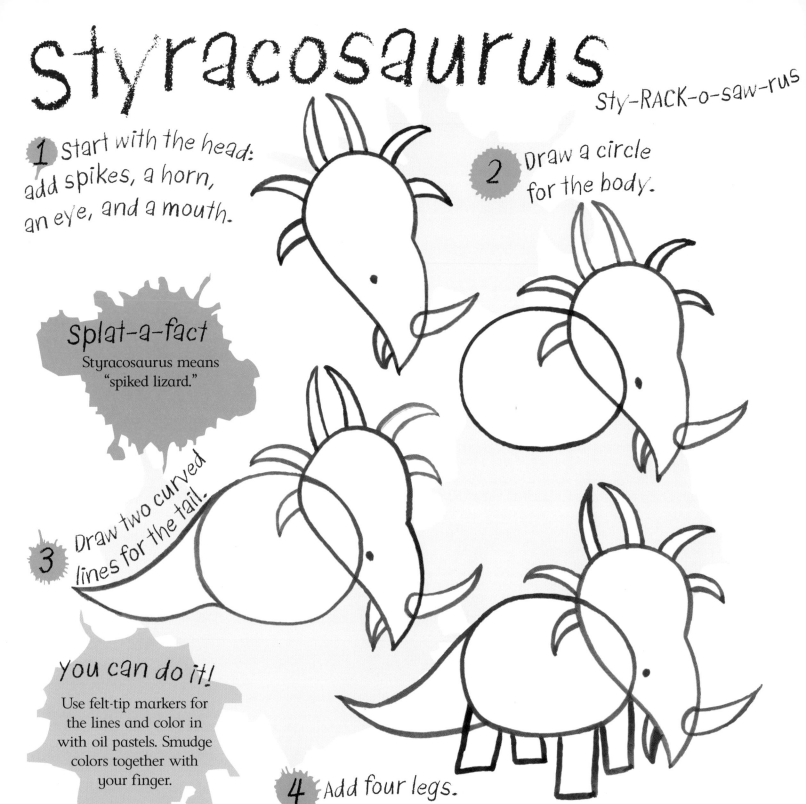

Velociraptor

Veh-LOSS-er-rap-tor

1 Start with the head and a dot for the eye.

2 Add nostril, mouth, and teeth.

3 Draw in two lines for the neck and an oval shape for the body.

4 Draw two lines for the tail and two arms.

You can do it!
Use felt-tip markers for the lines and add color usng colored pencils.

Splat-a-fact
Velociraptors starred in the film *Jurassic Park*.

5 Add two legs with clawed feet.

Triceratops

TRY-SERRA-tops

1 Start with the head and a dot for the eye.

2 Draw in horns and the mouth.

you can do it!

Use a felt-tip pen for the lines. Add color with watercolor or ink. Use crayons then paint on top. Make a smudge on the Triceratops by adding orange paint to the pink paint while it is still wet.

3 Draw in an oval shape for the body.

splat-a-fact

A Triceratops was almost twice the length of a rhinoceros.

4 Add four legs and draw two curved lines for the tail.

Corythosaurus

core-ith-o-SAW-russ

2 Add a nostril, the mouth, and an egg-shaped bump on top.

3 Draw two lines for the neck joined to a large oval shape.

1 Start with the head and add a dot for the eye.

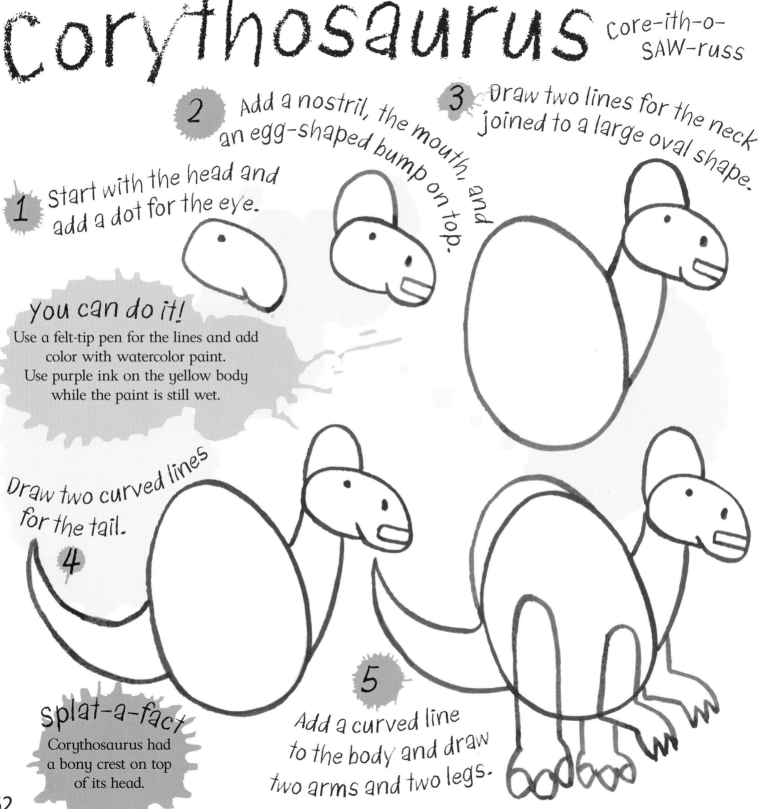

you can do it!
Use a felt-tip pen for the lines and add color with watercolor paint.
Use purple ink on the yellow body while the paint is still wet.

Draw two curved lines for the tail.

4

splat-a-fact
Corythosaurus had a bony crest on top of its head.

5 Add a curved line to the body and draw two arms and two legs.

Index